BIG PRESCHOOL WORKBOOK

AGES 3-5

LEARN LETTERS, NUMBERS, SHAPES, PATTERNS, AND MORE!

Copyright © 2017 by Dylanna Press
All rights reserved. This book or any portion thereof
may not be reproduced or used in any manner whatsoever without the express written permission of the publisher
except for the use of brief quotations in a book review.
First edition: 2017
Disclaimer/Limit of Liability
This book is for informational purposes only. The views expressed are those of the author alone, and should not
be taken as expert, legal, or medical advice. The reader is responsible for his or her own actions.
Every attempt has been made to verify the accuracy of the information in this publication. However, neither the
author nor the publisher assumes any responsibility for errors, omissions, or contrary interpretation of the material
contained herein.

Trace the Lines

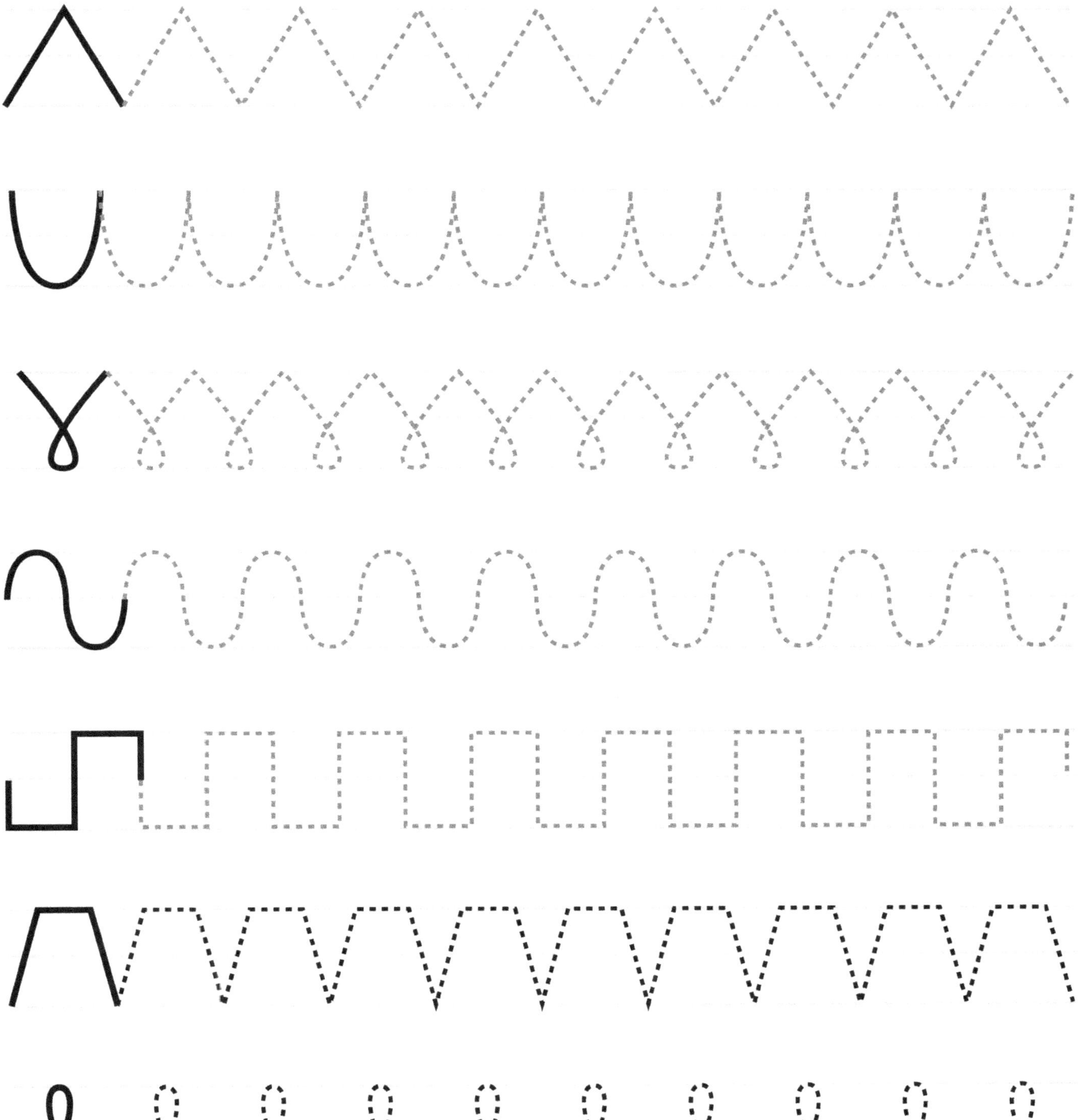

Trace & Color the Shapes

CIRCLE	SQUARE 	TRIANGLE

HEXAGON 	RECTANGLE 	QUATREFOIL

STAR 	DIAMOND 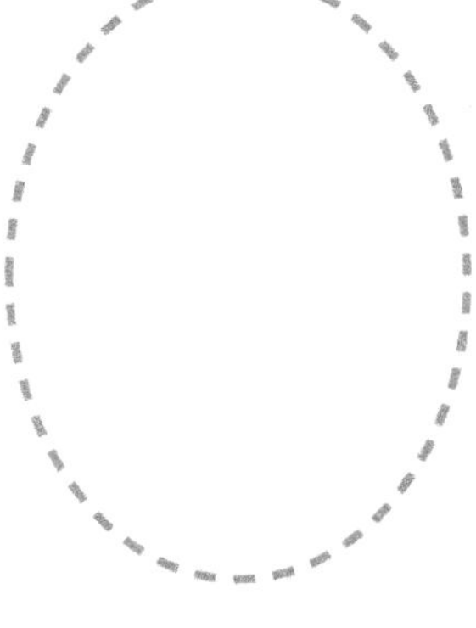	OVAL

Recognizing Shapes

Identify shapes that match exactly and color them with the same color

Color Similar Shapes

There are three similar pictures in each row, color them

Find the Biggest Shape

Find the biggest shape in each row and color it.

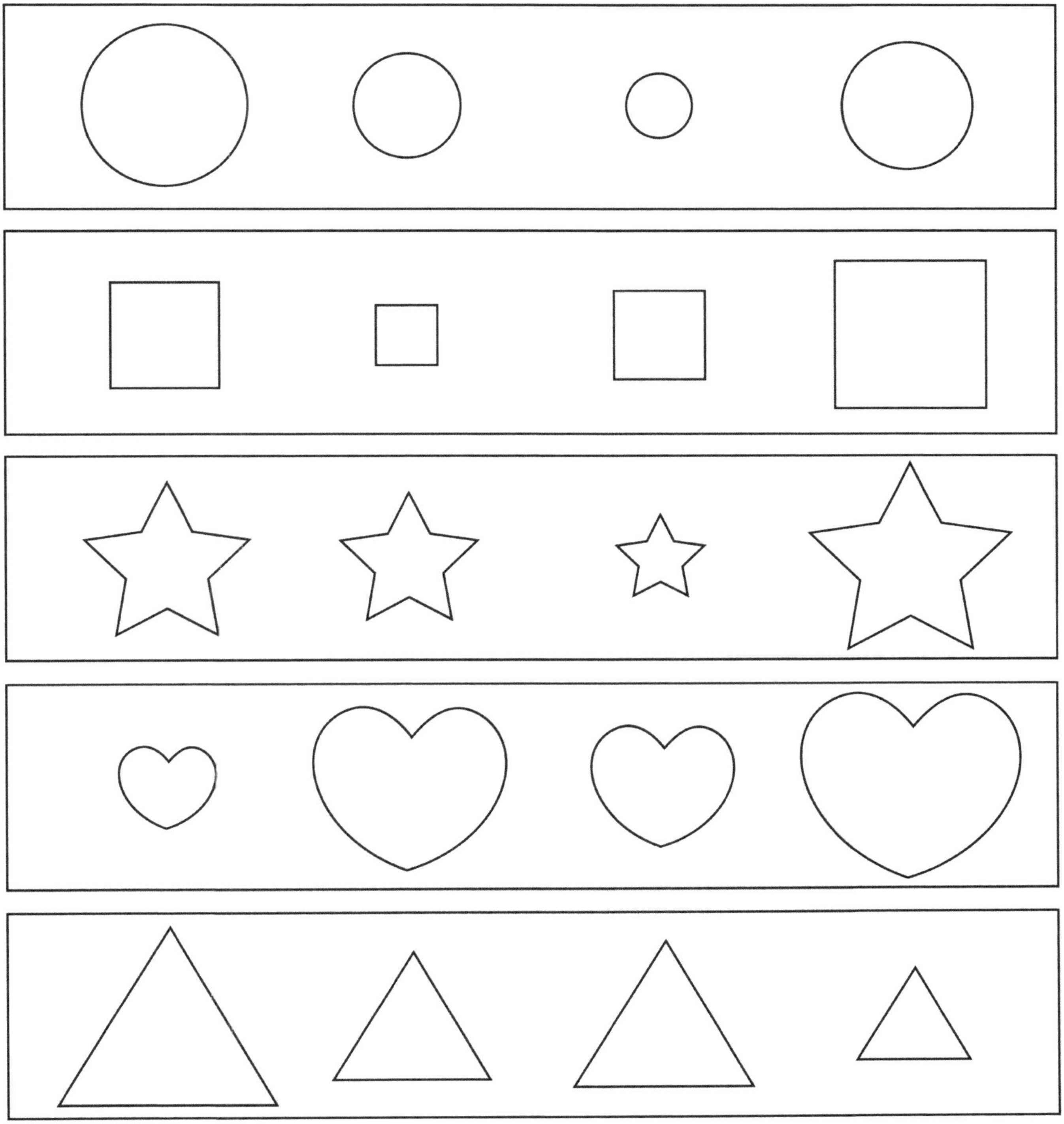

Find the Smallest Shape

Find the smallest shape in each row and color it.

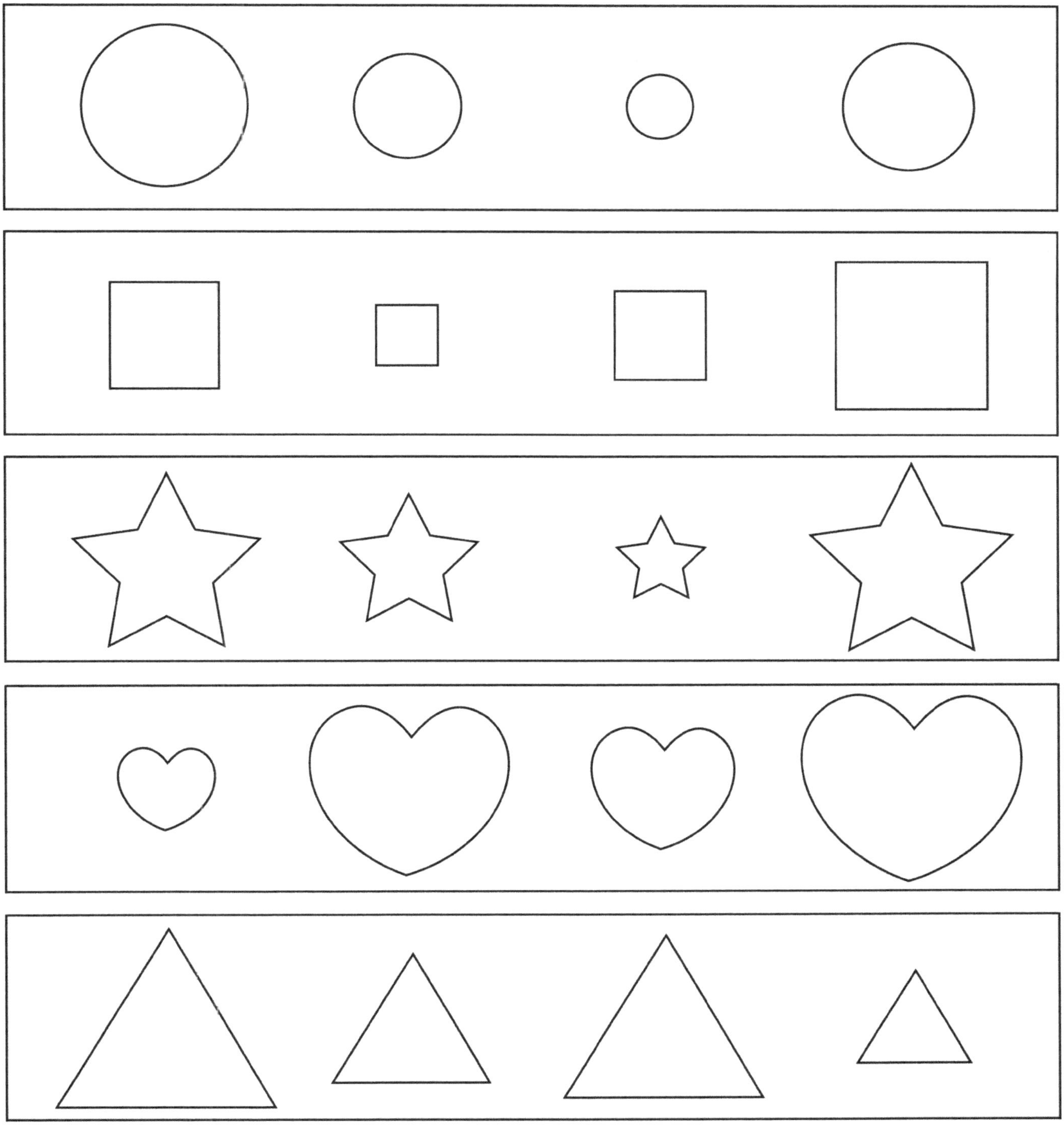

Find Similar Shapes

Count the similar shapes and write the number.

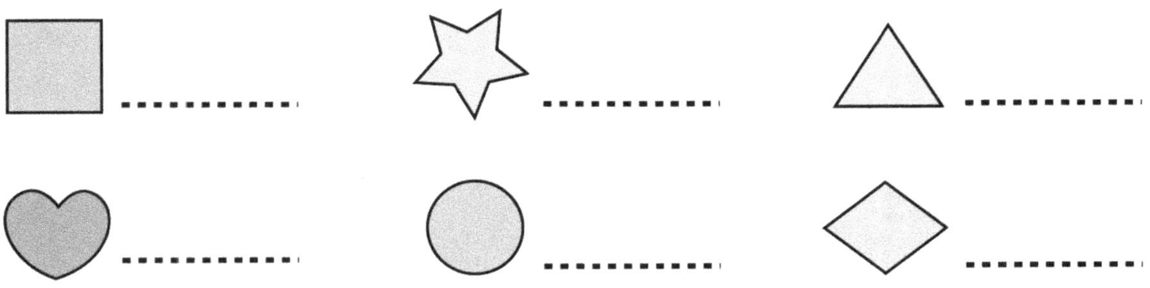

Match the Shapes

 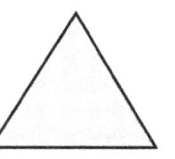

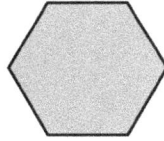 

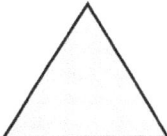 

 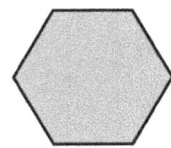

Trace the Shapes

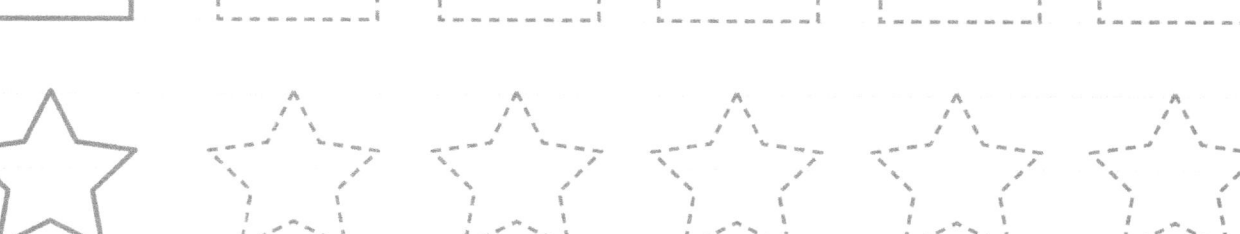
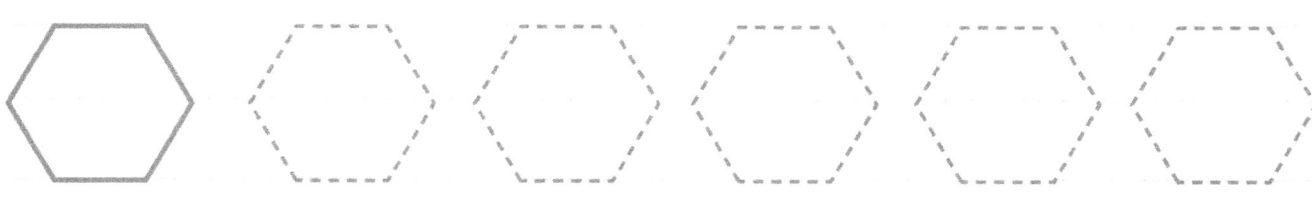
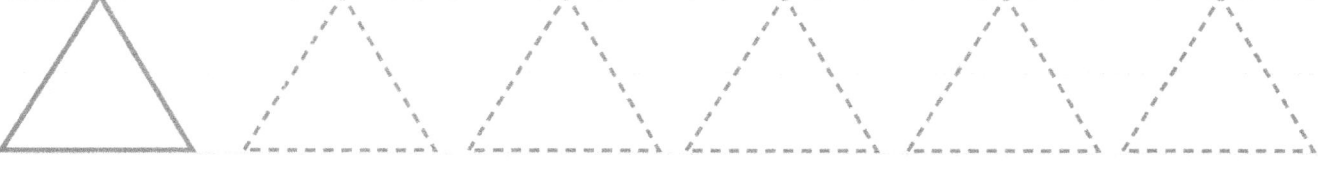
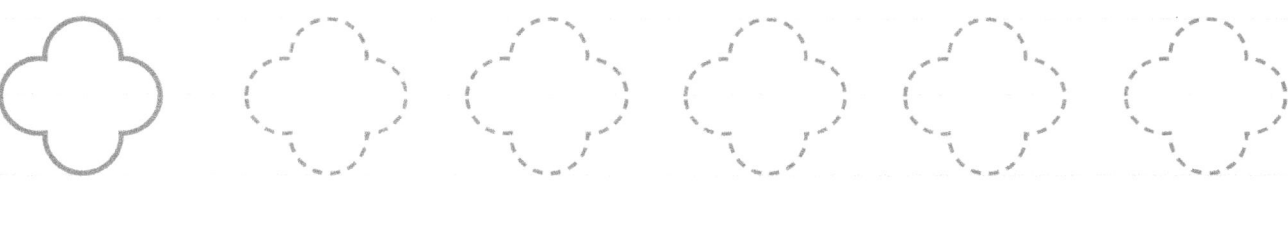
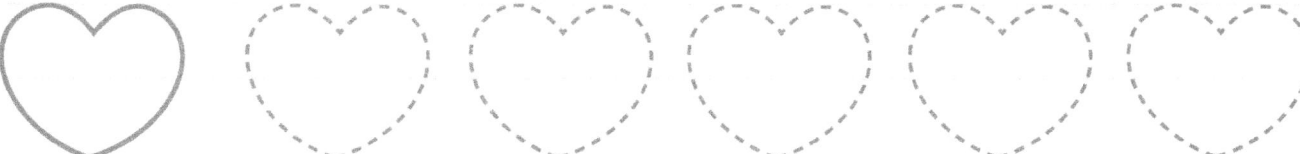

Match similar Shapes

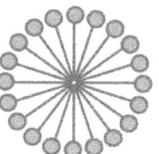

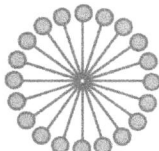

Identify and color the correct shape

Square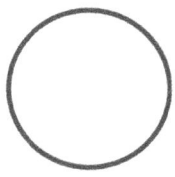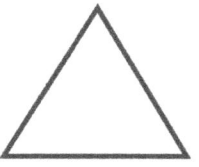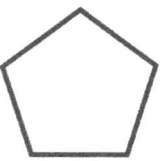

Circle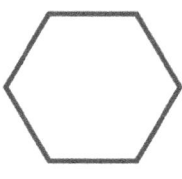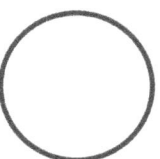

Heart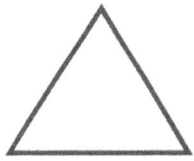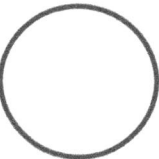

Triangle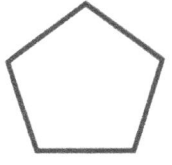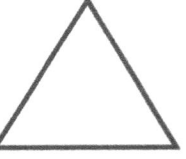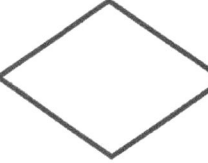

Oval

Star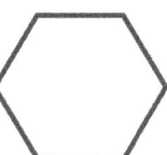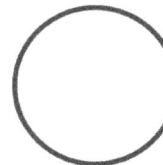

Name : ....

Recognizing Shapes

Draw a line to connect each picture with its other half.

Recognizing Patterns

What comes next? Circle the answer

1.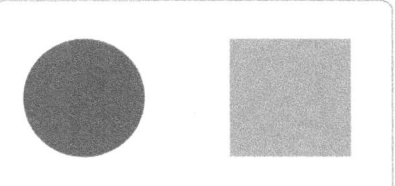

2.

3.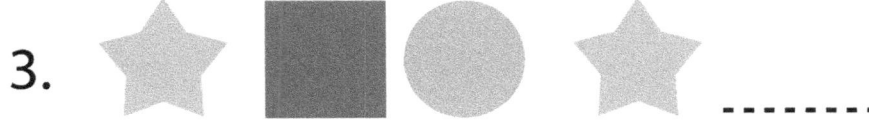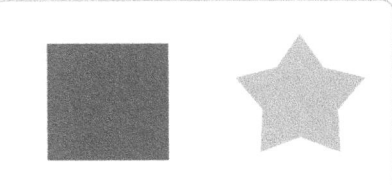

4.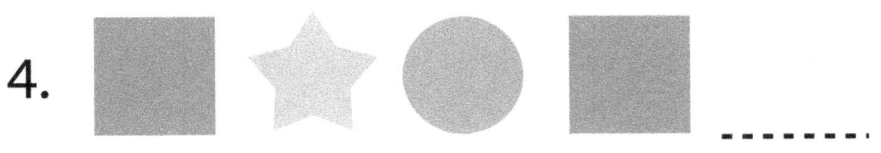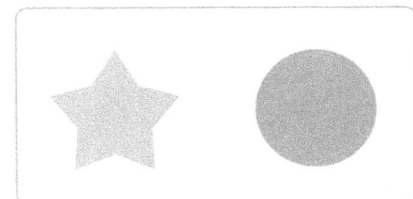

5.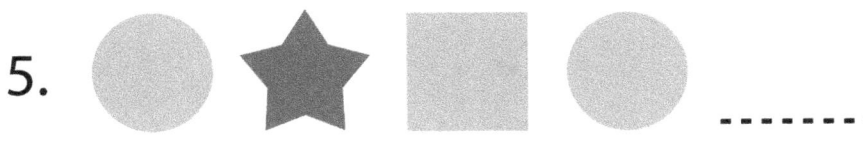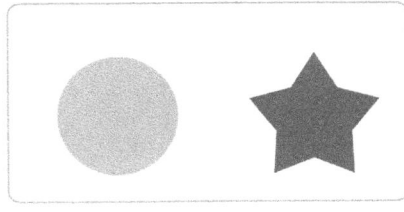

6.

WHAT COMES NEXT?

WHAT COMES NEXT?

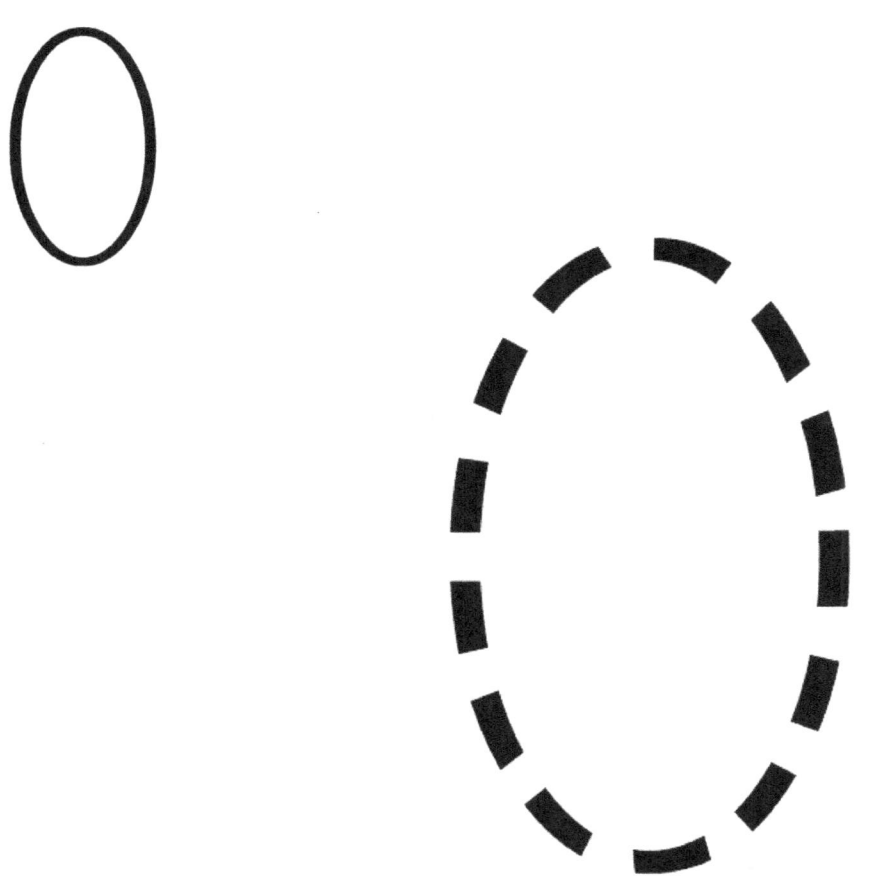

Trace the Os.

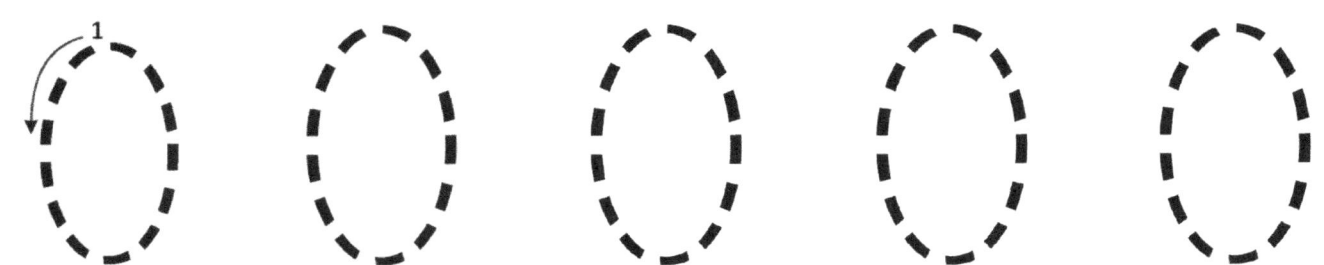

Trace the 1s.

Trace the 2s.

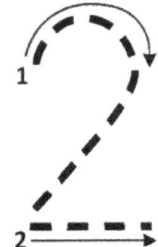    

3

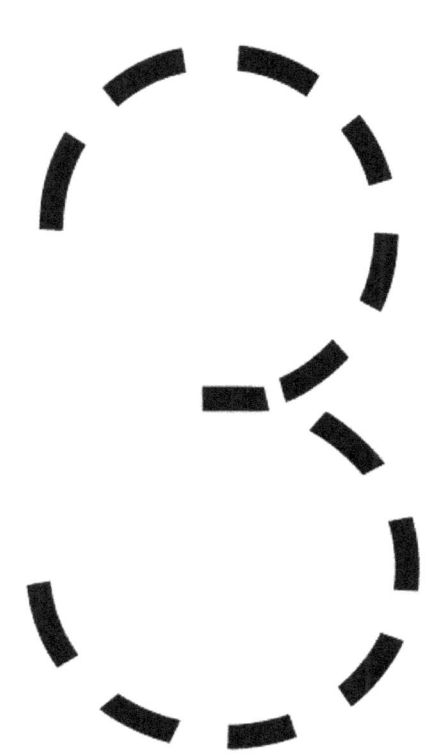

Trace the 3s.

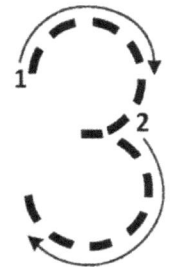    

Trace 4.

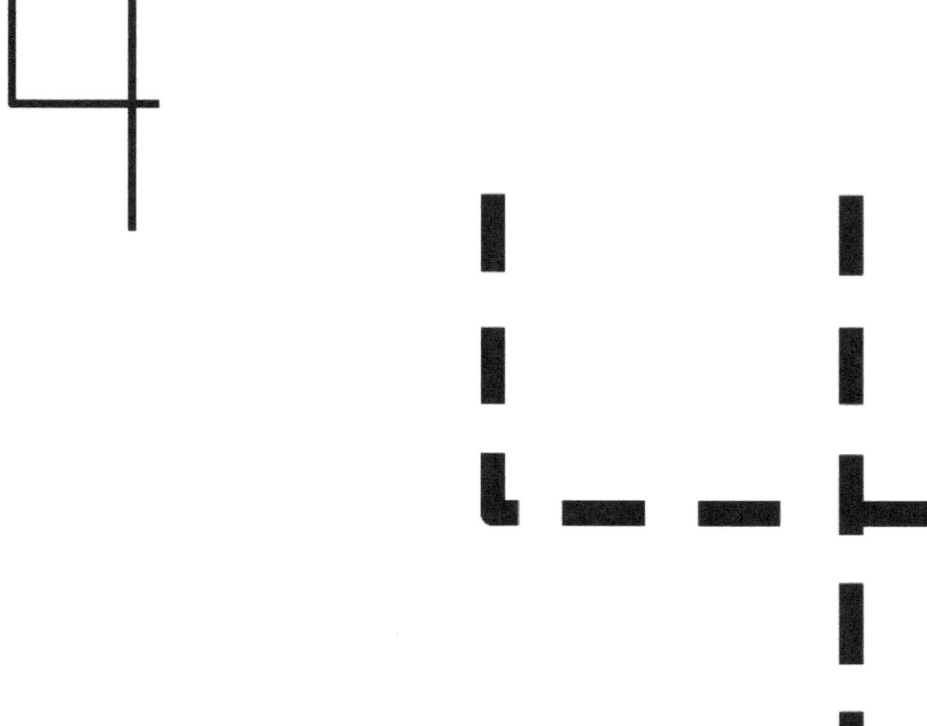

Trace the 4s.

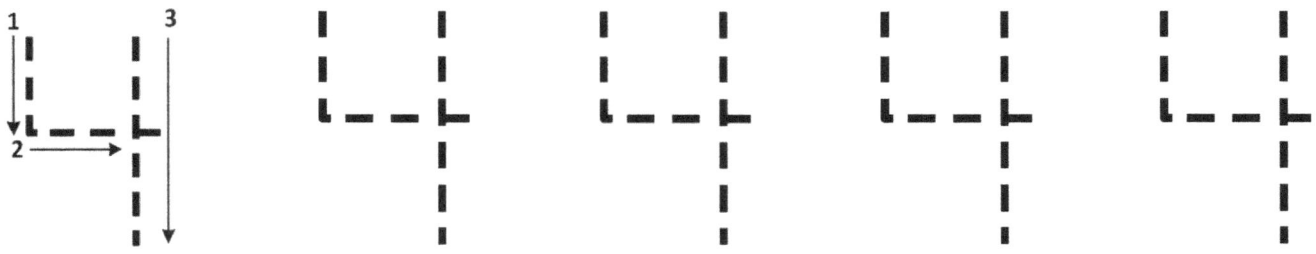

Trace the 5s.

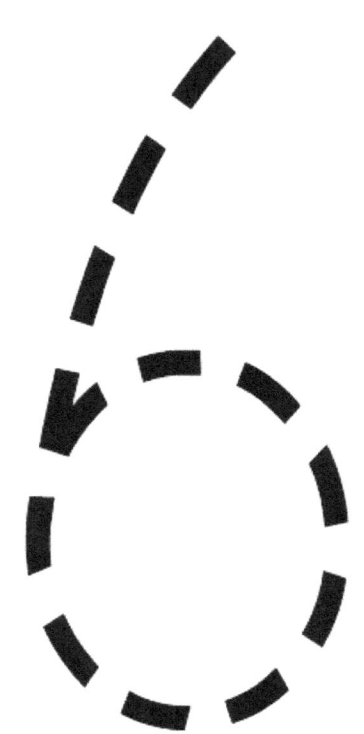

Trace the 6s.

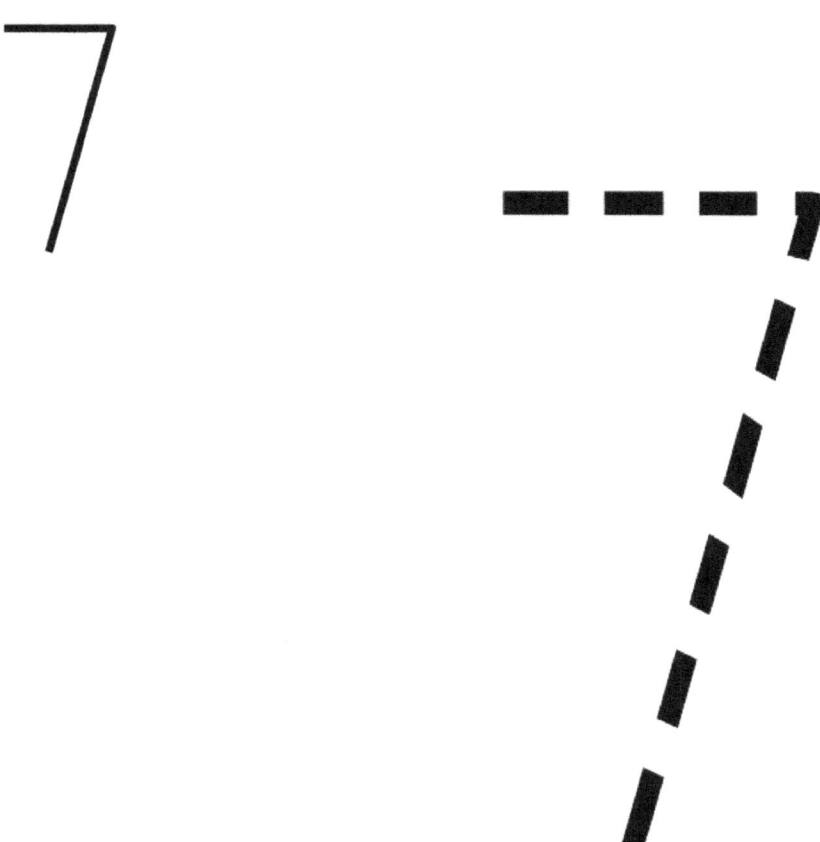

Trace the 7s.

Trace the 8s.

Trace the 9s.

Trace the 10s.

Dots					
●	1	1	1	1	1
● ●	2	2	2	2	2
● ● ●	3	3	3	3	3
● ● ● ●	4	4	4	4	4
● ● ● ● ●	5	5	5	5	5
● ● ● ● ● ●	6	6	6	6	6
● ● ● ● ● ● ●	7	7	7	7	7
● ● ● ● ● ● ● ●	8	8	8	8	8
● ● ● ● ● ● ● ● ●	9	9	9	9	9
● ● ● ● ● ● ● ● ● ●	10	10	10	10	10

Count and Write

Count the objects and write down the correct number on the box on your left

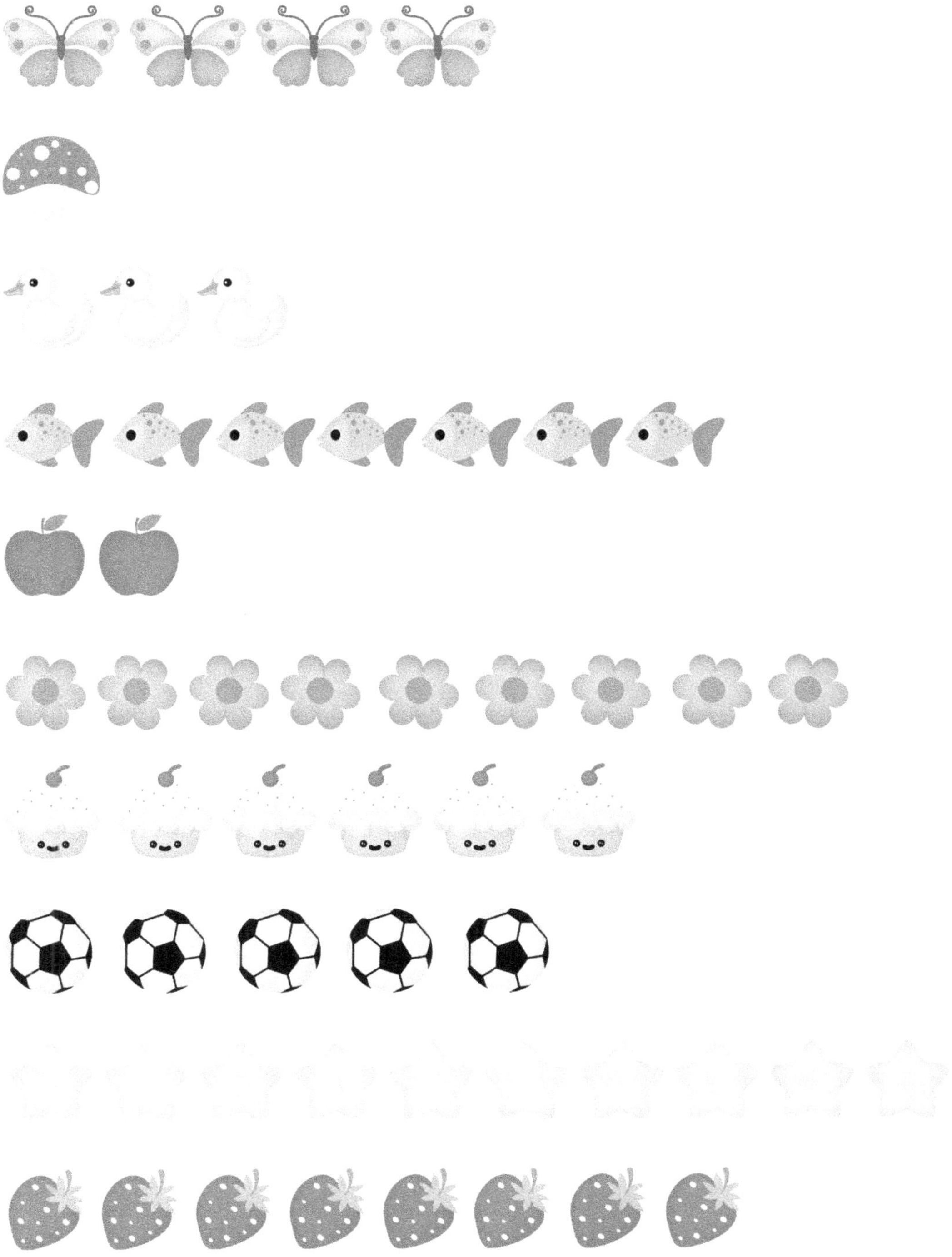

 **Match the fruits with the correct numbers**

 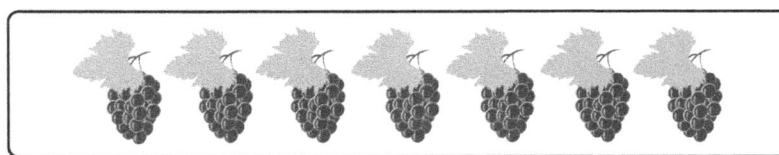

 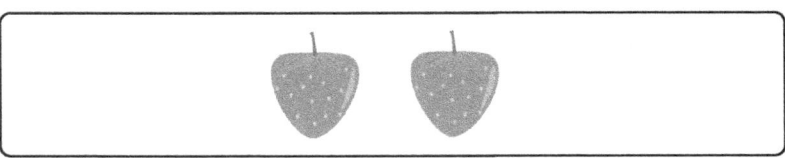

 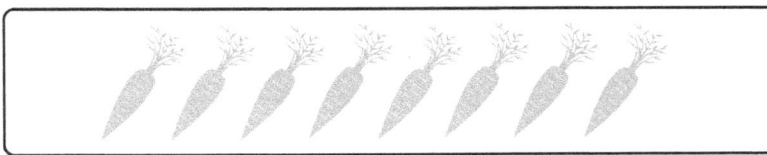

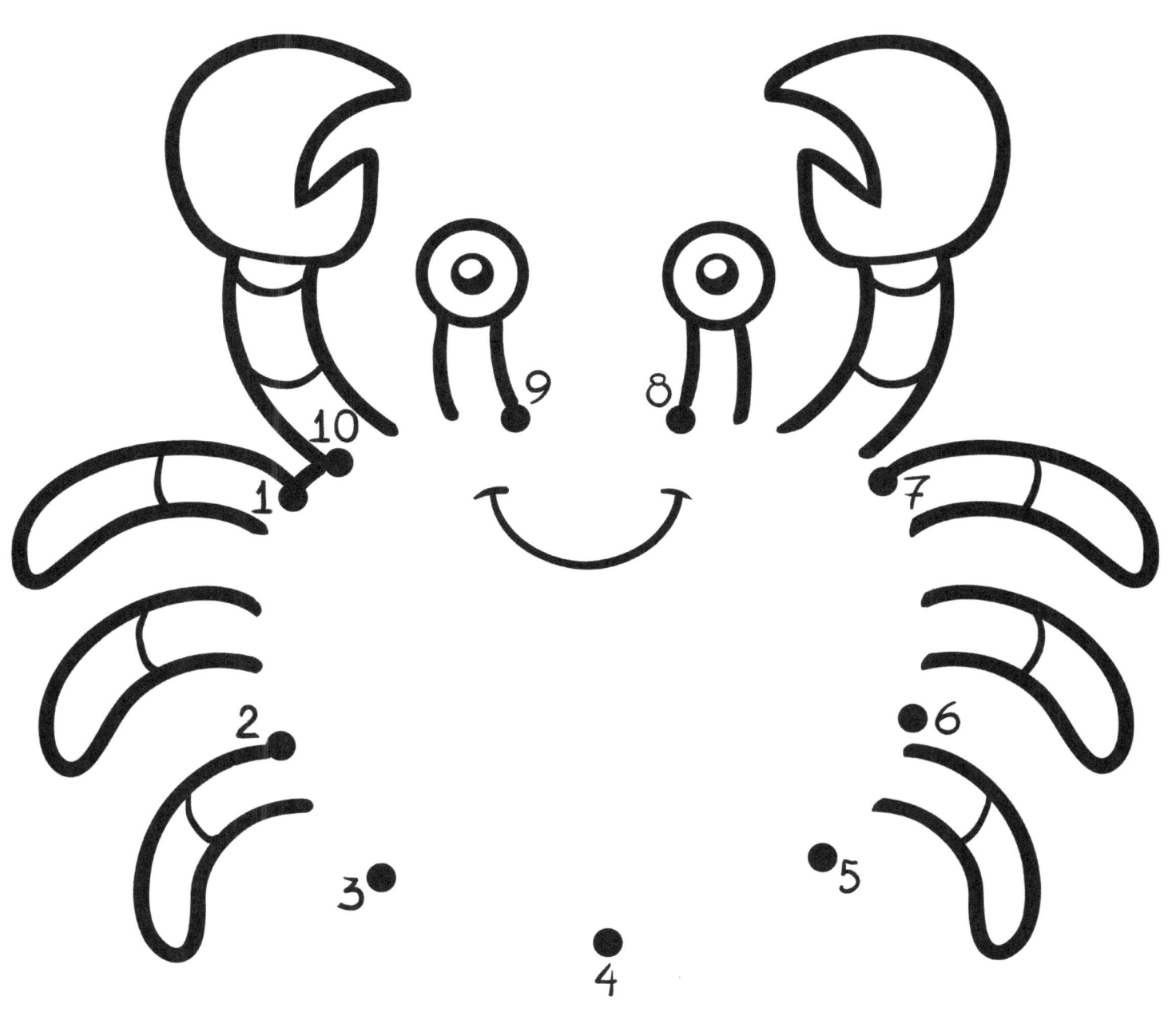

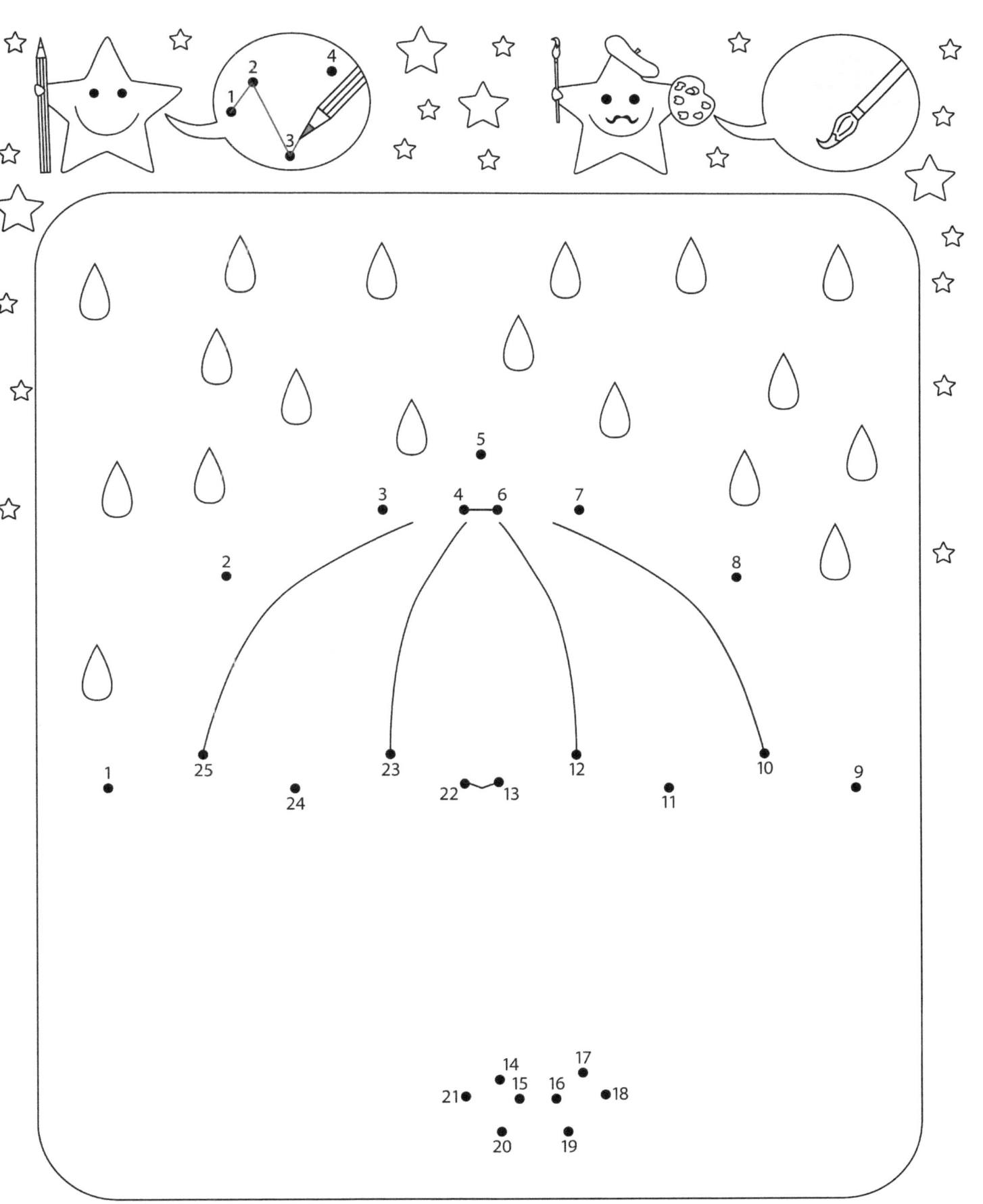

= light brown   2 = dark brown   3 = pink   4 = blue   5 = black

=yellow   2 = gray   3 = blue   4 = red

= green   2 = blue   3 = pink   4 =gray

= brown   2 = pink   3 = light brown   4 = orange

= yellow   2 = red   3 = blue   4 = gray

Let's help the mother cat to find her cub kitten

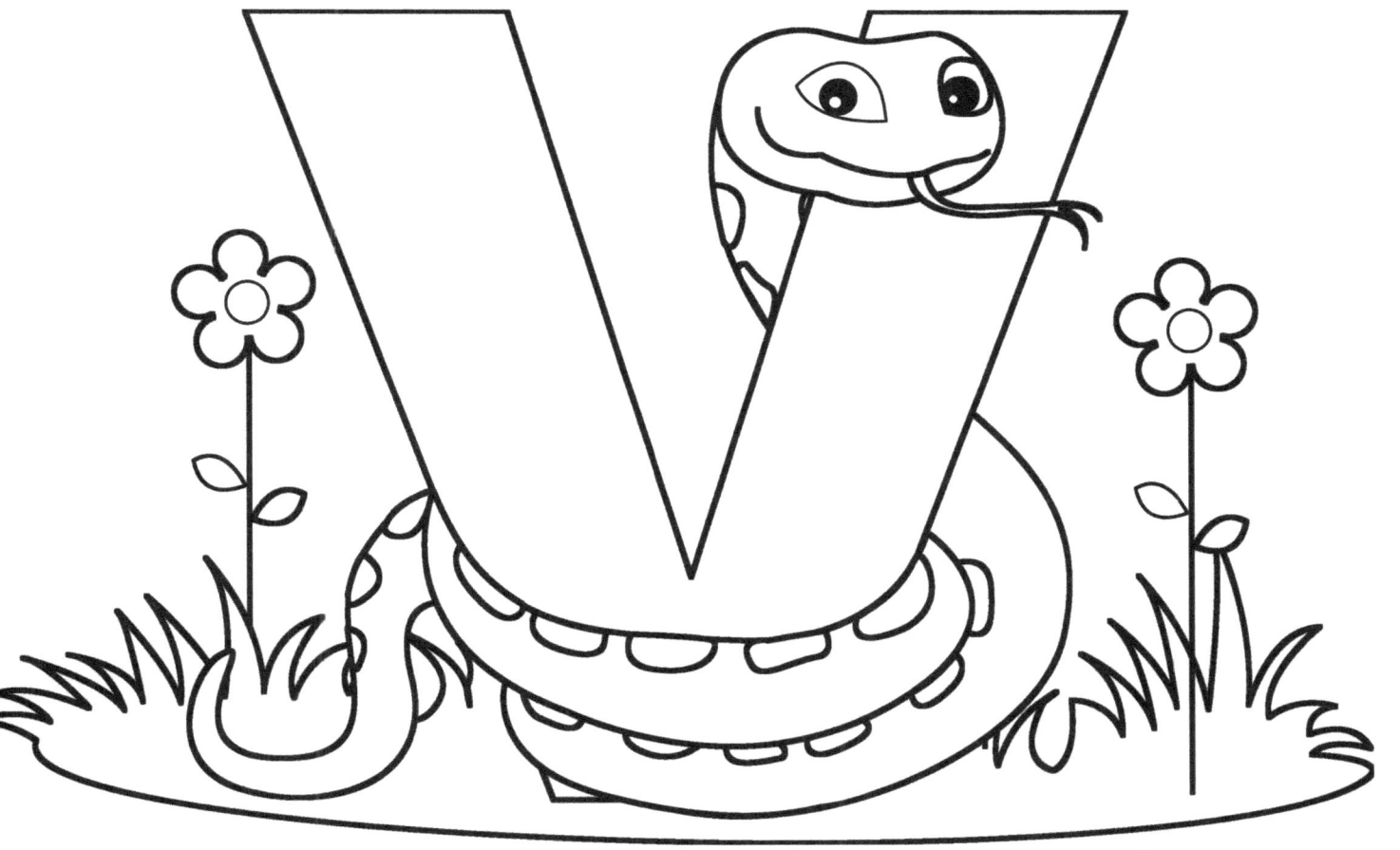

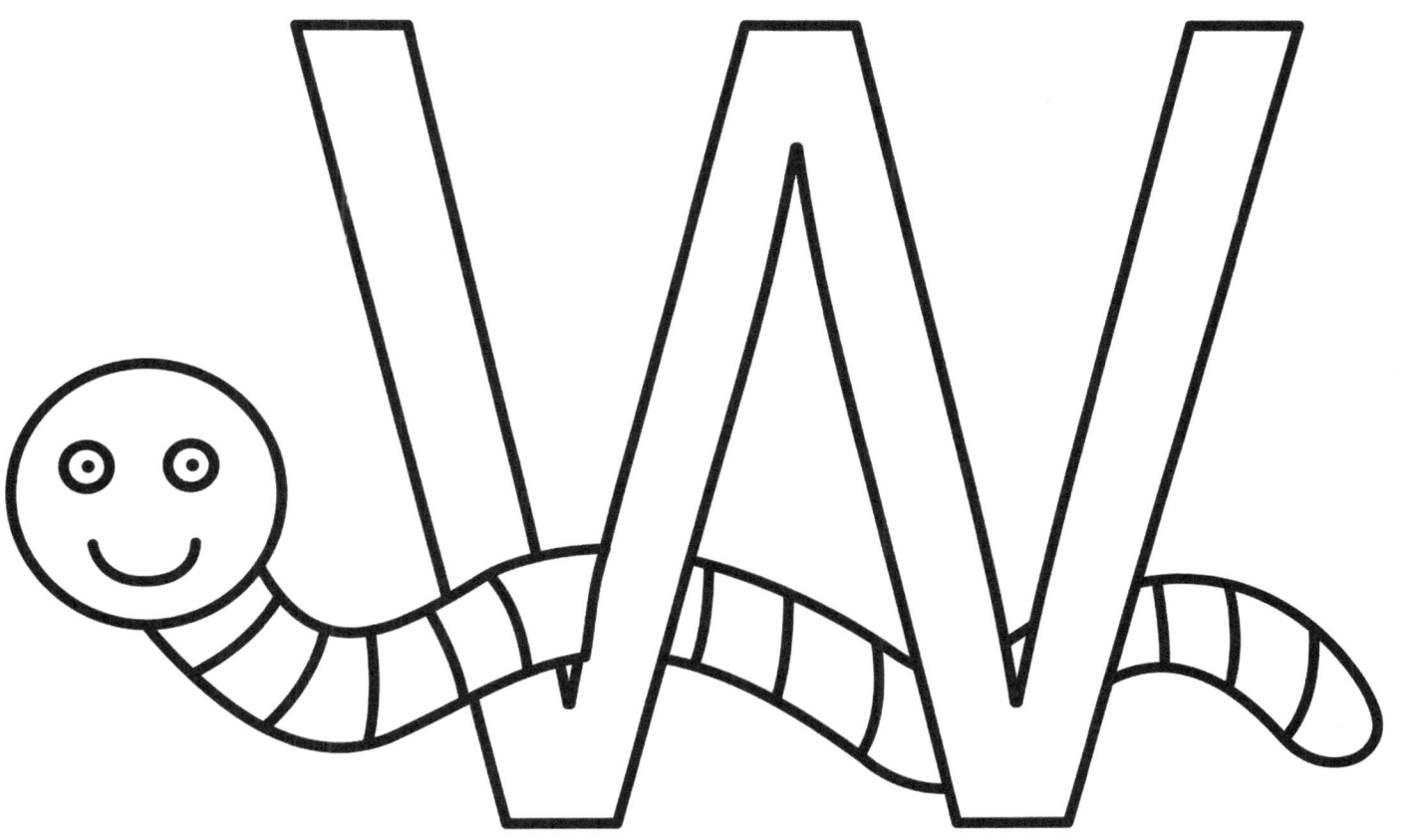

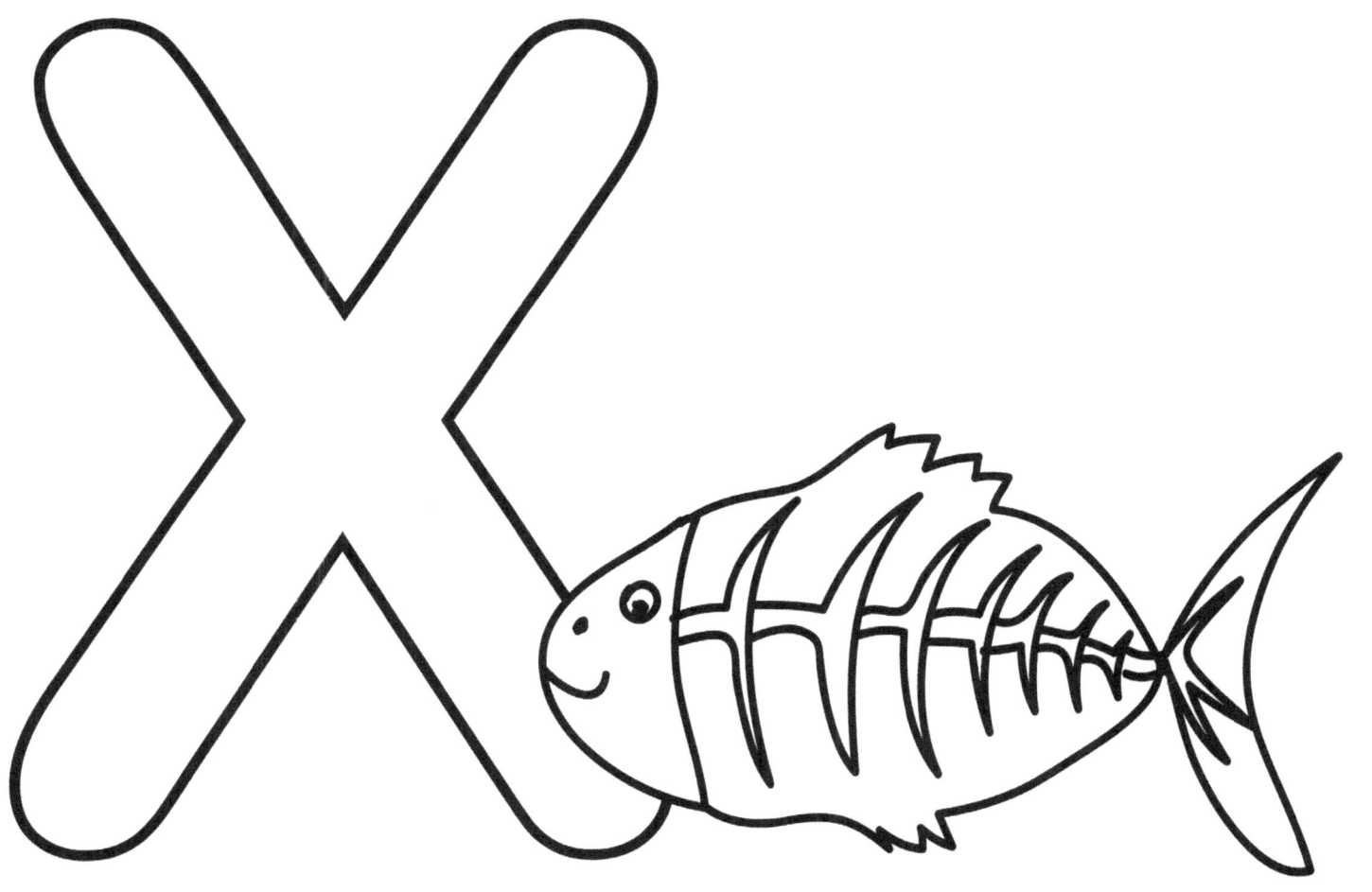

Writing Practice - Alphabet

Aa Bb Cc Dd Ee
Ff Gg Hh Ii Jj
Kk Ll Mm Nn
Oo Pp Qq Rr
Ss Tt Uu Vv
Ww Xx Yy Zz

Capital & Simple Letters

Color the shape with matching simple letter

1. B ⟶ c b d h
2. M ⟶ m n u v
3. G ⟶ y k g j
4. N ⟶ l n m u
5. H ⟶ i f n h
6. Q ⟶ g q c o
7. R ⟶ s c t r

Color the **Vegetables**

Match the creatures with their homes

FIND THE CORRECT SHADOW

Shadow Matching Game

- Color the pictures
- Draw the lines matching each picture to its shadow

African Animals

HOW MANY?

🐟 ☐   ✿ ☐   🐚 ☐   🐦 ☐

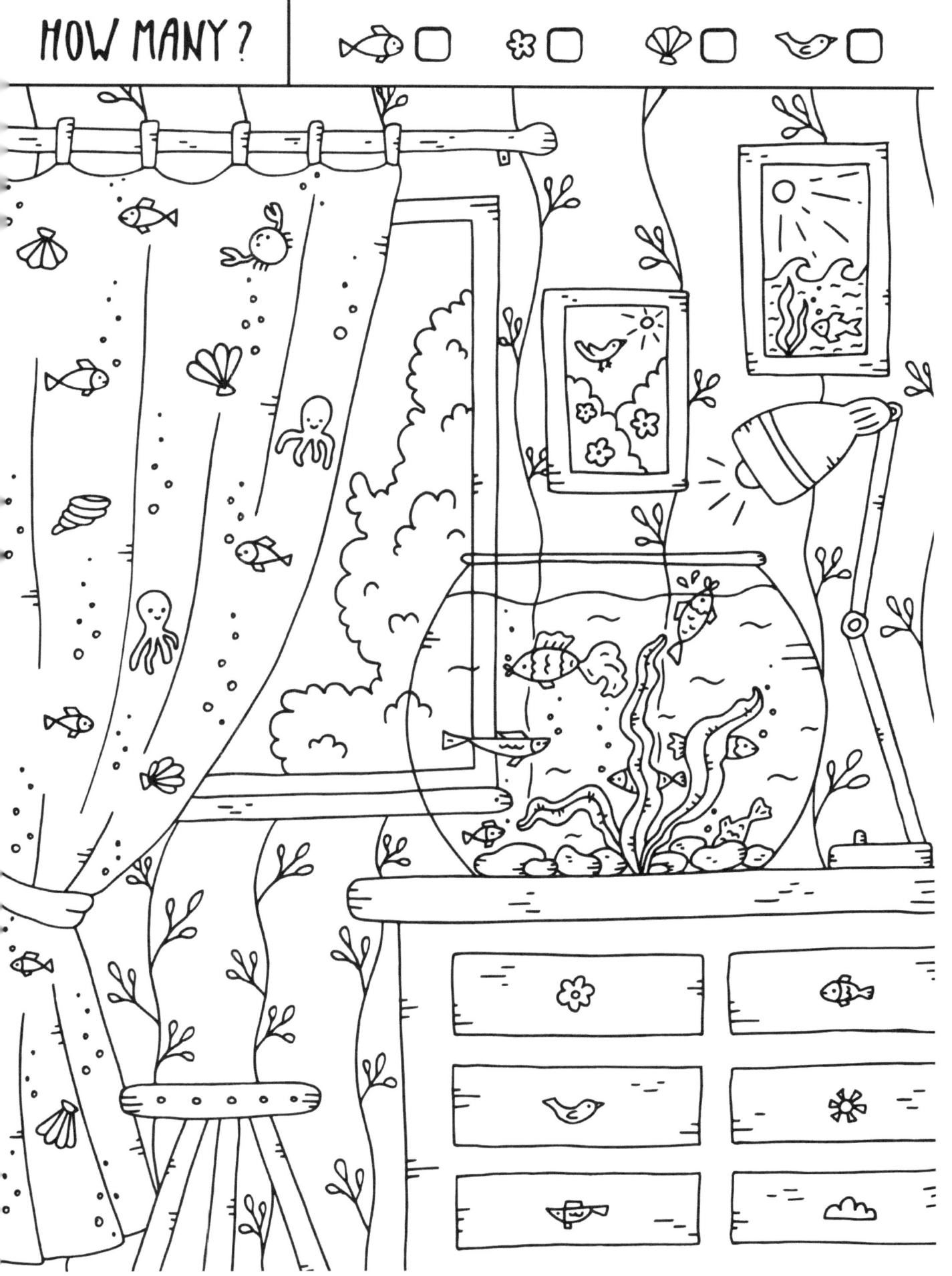

HOW MANY?

HOW MANY?

www.ingramcontent.com/pod-product-compliance
Lightning Source LLC
Chambersburg PA
CBHW081347080526
44588CB00016B/2405